IN THE GARDEN WITH
THE TOTTERINGS

ANNIE TEMPEST

FRANCES LINCOLN LIMITED

PUBLISHERS

Frances Lincoln Limited
4 Torriano Mews
Torriano Avenue
London NW5 2RZ
www.franceslincoln.com

In the Garden with the Totterings
Copyright © The O'Shea Gallery 2011
Text copyright © Annie Tempest 2011
Illustrations copyright © Annie Tempest 2011

Illustrations archived and compiled by
Raymond O'Shea

British Library Cataloguing in Publication Data
A catalogue record for this book is available from
the British Library.

ISBN 978-0-7112-3185-6

Printed in China
Bound for North Pimmshire

9 8 7 6 5 4 3 2

Other Tottering-by-Gently books by Annie Tempest:
Out and About with the Totterings
Drinks with the Totterings
The Totterings' Desk Diary
The Totterings' Pocket Diary
Tottering-by-Gently Annual
Available from Frances Lincoln at www.franceslincoln.com

At Home with the Totterings
Tottering-by-Gently Vol III
Available from The Tottering Drawing Room, along with a full range of
Tottering-by-Gently licensed product, at The O'Shea Gallery, No. 4 St James's Street,
London SW1A 1EF (Telephone +44 (0)207 930 5880) or www.tottering.com

I do think that on Mother's Day you lot might have made a bit more effort for me...

Serena

Freddy

Daisy

Gladys Shagpile

Scribble

Slobber

Hon Jon

THE O'SHEA GALLERY

Raymond O'Shea of The O'Shea Gallery was originally one of London's leading antiquarian print and map dealers. Historically, antiquarian galleries sponsored and promoted contemporary artists who they felt complemented their recognized areas of specialization. It was in this tradition that O'Shea first contacted *Country Life* magazine to see if Annie Tempest would like to be represented and sponsored by his gallery. In 1995 Raymond was appointed agent for Annie Tempest's originals and publisher of her books. Raymond is responsible for creating an archive of all of Annie's cartoons.

In 2003, the antiquarian side of his business was put on hold and the St. James's Street premises were finally converted to The Tottering Drawing Room at The O'Shea Gallery. It is now the flagship of a worldwide operation that syndicates and licenses illustrated books, prints, stationery, champagne, jigsaws, greetings cards, ties and much more. It has even launched its own fashion range of tweeds and shooting accessories under the label Gently Ltd.

The Tottering Drawing Room at The O'Shea Gallery is a wonderful location which is now available for corporate events of 45–125 people and is regularly used for private dinner parties catering for up to 14 people. Adjacent to St. James's Palace, the gallery lies between two famous 18th century shops: Berry Bros. & Rudd, the wine merchants and Locks, the hatters. Accessed through French doors at the rear of the gallery lies Pickering Place – not only the smallest public square in Great Britain, with original gas lighting, but it was also where the last duel in England was fought. A plaque on the wall, erected by the Anglo-Texan Society, indicates that from 1842–45 a building here was occupied by the Legation from the Republic of Texas to the Court of St. James.

Raymond O'Shea and Annie Tempest are delighted to be able to extend Tottering fans a warm welcome in the heart of historic St. James's where all the original Tottering watercolours can be seen along side a full product and print range.

TOTTERING-BY-GENTLY ®
ANNIE TEMPEST

Annie Tempest is one of the top cartoonists working in the UK. This was recognized in 2009 with the Cartoon Art Trust awarding her the prestigious Pont Prize for the portrayal of the British Character.

Annie's cartoon career began in 1985 with the success of her first book, *How Green Are Your Wellies?* This led to a regular cartoon, 'Westenders' in the *Daily Express*. Soon after, she joined the *Daily Mail* with 'The Yuppies' cartoon strip which ran for more than seven years and for which, in 1989, she was awarded 'Strip Cartoonist of the Year'. Since 1993 Annie Tempest has been charting the life of Daffy and Dicky Tottering in Tottering-by-Gently – the phenomenally successful weekly strip cartoon in *Country Life* magazine.

Daffy Tottering is a woman of a certain age who has been taken into the hearts of people all over the world. She reflects the problems facing women in their everyday life and is completely at one with herself, while reflecting on the intergenerational tensions and the differing perspectives of men and women, as well as dieting, ageing, gardening, fashion, food, field sports, convention and much more.

Daffy and her husband Dicky live in the fading grandeur of Tottering Hall, their stately home in the fictional county of North Pimmshire, with their extended family: son and heir Hon Jon, daughter Serena, and grandchildren, Freddy and Daisy. The daily, Mrs Shagpile, and love of Dicky's life, Slobber, his black Labrador, and the latest addition to the family, Scribble, Daisy's working Cocker Spaniel, also make regular appearances.

Annie Tempest was born in Zambia in 1959. She has a huge international following and has had eighteen one-woman shows, from Mexico to Mayfair. Her work is now syndicated from New York to Dubai and she has had numerous collections of her cartoons published. *In the Garden with the Totterings* is the latest to be published.

2010 © Garlinda Birkbeck

GREAT GARDENING MOMENTS...

...That mug of Earl Grey next to a barrow full of couch grass...

INTRODUCTION

One of the mysteries of Tottering Hall is its garden or park for we never learn of its extent. All we see are glimpses, vignettes of this or that corner. There's a kitchen garden, a clipped *parterre*, flights of steps and balustrading, a tree house, a green house, lush herbaceous borders, brick walls and miles of lawn – too many miles really. However we never learn of their relationship to each other or indeed the house. Perhaps Annie Tempest has that information tucked away somewhere, a plan of the domain of this aristocratic couple. Perhaps one day she will share it with the Tottering fan club.

His lordship we know does not share his wife's enthusiasm for things horticultural. His role is one of repose on a variety of deck chairs and garden seats – stirring himself only occasionally to make enough jam and preserves to supply a small army. Even so, he never arises beyond being an acolyte to Lady Tottering whose own approach to the garden is akin to that of a horticultural flame thrower. This is a chatelaine who weeds, plants, feeds, waters and loves her garden with a vengeance blasting it if it doesn't come up to scratch. Energy and lethargy seize her with equal force as Lady Tottering does nothing by halves.

The Tottering Hall garden has one other central mystery, for I can't believe that it is maintained without the help of an opposite to Mrs Shagpile inside. Who and where is that person? Perhaps it is time for Annie Tempest to add another character to her irresistible cast.

Sir Roy Strong

THE PLEASURE OF GARDENING

...Being pricked by thorny things...

...Being stung by stinging things...

...Being stuck to by sticky things...

...Being bitten by buzzy things...

Just
get
me
a LARGE
glass of wine
and
nobody
gets hurt...

Marvellous natural remedy! She says it beats HRT hands down...

I've just got to pop down to the garden centre, darling...

We went yesterday! What on earth do you need this time?

I don't know 'til I get there...

No, no - tell me, darling - you know I'm always dying to hear all about what ever you've been up to in the garden...

THE PERFECT MARRIAGE

Being supportive...

THE PERFECT MARRIAGE

making time to listen to each other...

THE PERFECT MARRIAGE

dealing with problems together...

THE PERFECT MARRIAGE

keeping active in the bed department...

TUBS & POTS...

Shape, pollard and lop...

"If I haven't made a million by eighteen, then I'll just have to go into something my parents approve of..."

For heavens sake, Freddy — you're driving me mad!

Motherhood, eh! We spend the first few years of our kids lives' teaching them to walk and talk...

...then the next few longing for them to sit down and shut up...

ANNIE TEMPEST © 1999

"I wandered lonely as a cloud,
That floats on high o'er vales and hills,

When all at once I saw a crowd,
A host, of past it daffodils;

Amidst each clump, the nettles squeeze,
And cleavers cling there in the breeze..."

Annie Tempest © 2004

"I know I <u>said</u> I was only going to look but it's a woman's prerogative to change her mind, darling..."

I'm feeling really energetic today! I'm going to tackle those out-buildings. Get them sorted out!

...or maybe not...

Right! Today: Fork over borders, strim edges, water greenhouse and feed pots...

...and SBK nettles, Barrier H ragwort, set mole traps and pick the rocket...

I'm quite exhausted just thinking about it...

ANNIE TEMPEST © 2001

"What's the point of all your hard work in the garden if I'm not allowed to sit down and enjoy it..."

I spend hours trying to keep it all under control - pruning, thinning out, weeding... Dicky's a member of the NGS, you see...

Oh, yes - National Gardens Scheme?

No. Non Gardening Spouses.

Never too old to... play on the swings...

Never too old to... climb trees...

Gardening would be a lovely hobby for you to take up, Freddy-keep you away from those violent computer games...

sowing seeds, nurturing the seedlings, planting them out...watching them flower...

...and when they're old-chopping their heads off...

MULTIPURPOSE POTTING COMPOST

2003© ANNIE TEMPEST

The sun's out and the bluebells in the woods are looking lovely...

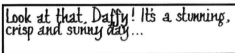

Look at that, Daffy! It's a stunning, crisp and sunny day...

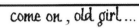

come on, old girl...

...let's go out and shoot something...

" There's another mole hill on my lawn...."

FEMALE SOLUTIONS : Molehills on the lawn...

Conversation.   Gossip

That's an awfully risky shot to take so early in the weekend...

"I think it only became a spectator sport when James got his little red tractor..."

Nearly finished, Dicky! This should be the last cut of the year...

I doubt it. You've just gone over the entire lawn without the blades on...

I think that book Serena had about men being from a different planet might have been right...
Kellogg's CORN FLAKES
FINANCIAL TIMES
TRADED OPTIONS
How could you not notice that the Snowdrops and Aconites are up this morning?...
1998 © ANNIE TEMPEST
Probably in the same way that you havent noticed that the Nikkei and FTSE are up, too...

Mars and Venus mow the lawn...

Oh! It's beautiful! You're so lucky - Dicky never buys me presents these days...

What?! How can you say that, Daffy? Only last week I bought you a lovely present...

A ragwort fork's not quite in the same league, Dicky...

ANNIE TEMPEST © 200

GREAT GARDENING MOMENTS . . . KNOWING THE LATIN NAME . . .

Oh! My Goodness! Corky Meadowgrass said he was going to move those bricks... the garden is open for the National Garden Scheme tomorrow.

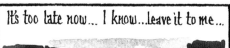

It's too late now... I know...leave it to me...

There - now it's an art intallation...

LADY TOTTERINGS UNMADE SHED

What do you do about your bindweed, Daffy?

There's only one thing you can do...

...call it Convolvulus and enjoy the flowers...

I've tried a fierce scarecrow, dangling Daily Mail CD's everywhere, planting plastic windmills and companion planting...

What else can I do if I want to stay organic and not have everything I plant attacked from all directions?..

Well – I thought it was worth a try...

POLITE NOTICE!
NO RABBITS,
PIGEONS,
SLUGS,
FLYING INSECTS
OR
SNAILS
IN VEGETABLE
GARDEN!
Thankyou!

Morning, Dotty! No, you didn't wake me - I'm in the rose garden...

...feeling rather like they look this morning...

...browned off and hung over with huge hips...

Yes – what are you hovering about for, Dicky?

I was just wondering why the herbaceous border gets breakfast before I do...

Remember Simon and Bella, mum? Always wolfing down steak tartare...

...they're now vegetarian health freaks...

...even their coffee-table books are decaffeinated...

1995 © ANNIE TEMPEST.

'Otsukushi! Mitsu-bachi ya ari wa kesshite namake-nai...'

Mr Okoshi say: 'beautiful! Bees and ants are never idle...'

Well, tell him, Dicky and I did most of the work, thank you very much...

Very original planting on this side. Is it some new look you saw at Chelsea Flower Show?

No that's my grandaughter's idea. She's delegated the design to her working Cocker...

... every time he digs a hole, she puts a plant in it...

At our age we should be doing Sudoku puzzles or at the very least a daily dementia check...

...apparently, you start at 100 and subtract 7 as many times and as quickly as you can.

OK. Where's the calculator?.

THE INDULGENT HOUSE GUEST...
...of family with budding one day eventer toddler...

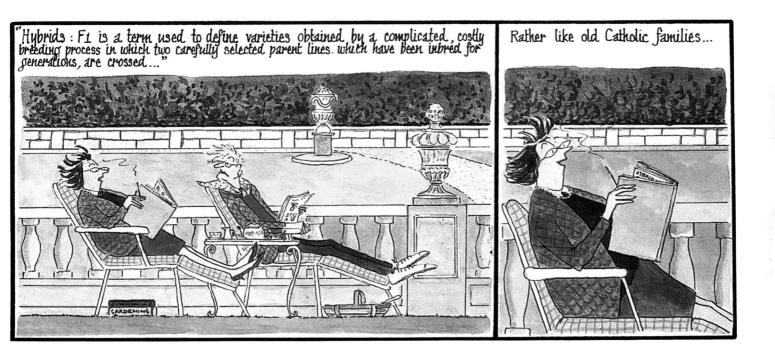

"Hybrids: F1 is a term used to define varieties obtained by a complicated, costly breeding process in which two carefully selected parent lines, which have been inbred for generations, are crossed..."

Rather like old Catholic families...

Raspberry Jam
4lbs raspberries
4lbs preserving sugar
knob of butter
Put the raspberries in Jam saucepan + simmer,
stirring occasionally, for 20 mins.
Take off heat & add sugar stirring until dissolved.
Add knob of butter & boil rapidly for half an hour.
Test for set. Stand for 15 mins. Pot.

Strawberry Jam
3½ lbs strawbs
3 tbsp. lemon juice
3 lbs preserving sugar
knob butter.
Put strawbs in pan with lemon juice & simmer,
stirring occasionally for 25 mins. Take off heat &
add sugar. Stir until dissolved. Add butter &
bring to boil rapidly for 20 mins.
Test for set. Stand for 15 mins. Pot.

It's a breath-taking garden, darling - but is it designed for easy maintainance?

Oh, yes absolutely, Daffy...

...by a brace of full-time, Kew-trained experts...

ANNIE TEMPEST © 1997

" I hope the windows are insured on your village church..."

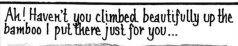

Look at that! Perfect weather! Not too hot. No rain forecast 'til tomorrow...

Ah! Haven't you climbed beautifully up the bamboo I put there just for you...

Sorry! Bindweed just brings out the devil in me...

SYSTEMIC WEED KILLER

Anne Tempest © 2009

Having a good day, Dicky?

Couldn't be better, Daffy – the fish haven't bothered me once...

I did warn you that I was a bit of a Cinderella on the tennis court - odds are against me ever getting to the ball...

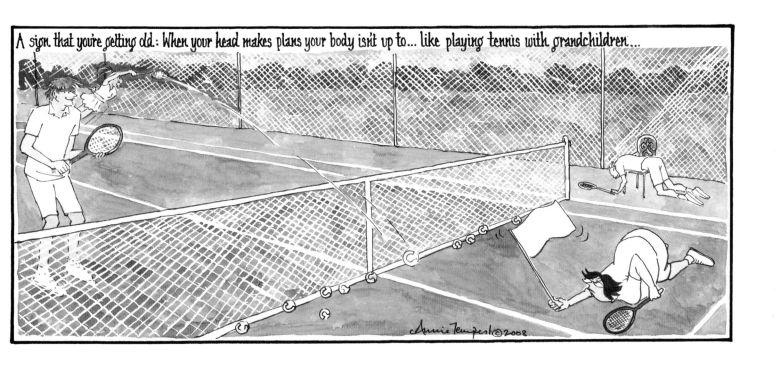

A sign that you're getting old: When your head makes plans your body isn't up to... like playing tennis with grandchildren...

Annie Tempest © 2008

My goodness! The garden has exploded into bloom! The Maigold is covered in roses...

Amazing what a drop of rain and a warm spell can do for the flowers...

Ah!... and the weeds...

Our first organic carrot, Dicky...

DAFFY PREPARES FOR BATTLE

ok! weeds - I'm coming to get you!...

One small nettle...   One GIANT...   ...network of rhizomes...

I think Mum's finally lost the plot with the ground Elder...

MOLE SMOKES!

"Are you sure you didn't mean 'Ground Elder shall inherit the earth ...'?"

ANNIE TEMPEST © 2001

" Was there any Bloody Horsetail in the garden of Eden, Granny ?... "

I wonder what 6-bedroom, Georgian houses around Farnham went for 100 years ago...

Were there any, Serena?...

...100 years ago I think Surrey was still our vegetable patch...

1997©ANNE TEMPEST.

WEEPING STANDARD

A SCARIFYING RAKE . . .

F1 HYBRID...   AN ARISTOCRATIC CLIMBER OF CONSIDERABLE QUALITY...

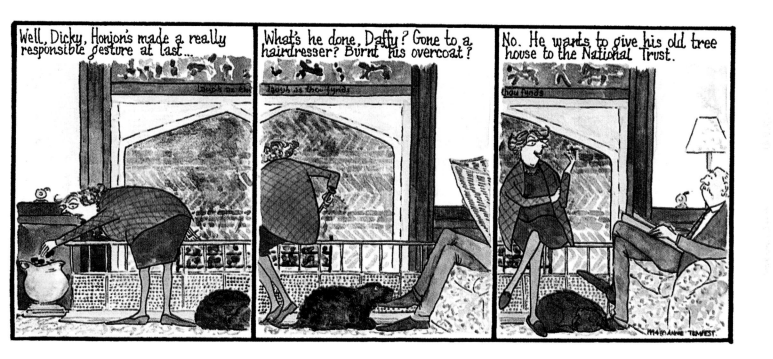

An old poorly shaped specimen....

Architectural shrubs...

Disappointing bedding varieties...

Darling, I love the fact that you've taken to making jams, jellies and pickles...it's just that I don't think we'll live long enough to get through this lot...

THE THREE AGES OF WOMAN...

HORSES

HORMONES

HORTICULTURE

CLOSING DOWN THE GARDEN FOR WINTER...

There's always something stinging you, pricking you or getting stuck to you...

I'm very sorry but you'll have to go back — you're trespassing!

But it says here that a pre-Saxon right of way runs through here...

That was only for bears, wolves and Romans whose chariots broke down...

Colder inside than out again, Mrs Shagpile...

1997 © ANNIE TEMPEST

Panel 1: Wouldn't it be lovely to be an Azalia, Lady Tottering...

Panel 2: No need for anti-wrinkle creams or hair-dyes...

Panel 3: We could just have our heads chopped off when we started getting dowdy and they'd grow back full of youthful bloom....

I'm not sure that giving Corky Meadowgrass a free hand is such a good idea, Daffy